The Blood of Dracula

Chris Bond

Series Editor: Andy Kempe

Nelson Thornes

This new edition published in 1999 by:
Stanley Thornes (Publishers) Ltd
Delta Place
27 Bath Road
CHELTENHAM GL53 7TH
England

11 / 10 9 8 7

A catalogue record for this book is available from the British Library.

ISBN 978-0-7487-4063-5

Printed and bound in Great Britain by Berforts Group

C O N T E N T S

SuperScripts

SuperScripts is a series of plays for use in the English classroom and the Drama Studio. The plays have been written by professional writers who share a delight in live performance and the challenges it offers to actors, designers, directors and, of course, audiences.

Most of the plays in the series were written for professional companies. All are included because they tell stories and use techniques which will interest, excite and offer new insights to young people who are just coming to understand how drama works as an art form.

The range of plays in the series addresses the requirement to give students at Key Stages 3 and 4 an opportunity to study a variety of dramatic genres. The fact that they were all written for performance (and have indeed all been performed) means that they will give students the chance to understand how and why playscripts are different from novels. The Activities presented after the script are designed to draw attention to this, and extend students' abilities in reading, writing and of course performing drama.

Many of the tasks invite students to engage directly with the text or formulate their own creative responses. Others focus on discussing, writing and designing. Both English and Drama specialists will find the series a valuable resource for promoting dramatic literacy – and simply performing the plays wouldn't be a bad thing either!

The Blood of Dracula

A quick whiz around any bookshop or video store will show you that there's money to be made in blood-sucking! Vampirism is big business. Publications range from children's picture books to adult novels and all manner of macabre and purportedly 'factual' material. Between 1957 and 1972 alone, more than two hundred vampire movies were made around the world. The story of Dracula has made household names of actors such as Bela Lugosi, Peter Cushing and Christopher Lee. Outside of theatre history, Bram Stoker (who worked for the great Victorian actor Sir Henry Irving) is probably only remembered for this one novel, and Vlad Dracul is certainly the only fifteenth-century Wallachian prince most of us are likely to have heard about.

It's not difficult to understand why the story continues to capture the imagination. The ability to transform one's shape, fly, and live forever are the stuff of common day-dreams for all ages. On another level, the stories may be seen as mixing the supernatural with adventure, and primordial fear with deep sexual urges. The recent Francis Ford Coppola version gave a new twist by depicting Dracula as being driven by passion rather than just lust.

Like all myths, the vampire has taken on a symbolic value. Perhaps the Victorians' fascination with the story says something about the repression of that age. A century later, the consequences of mixing blood and sex has other truly frightening implications.

Chris Bond's play draws on both the long history of the story and theatrical tradition. His version is self-mocking, almost a pantomime. It is unashamedly sexy, yet skilfully retains the excitement of a gothic melodrama. But it is also a play for our time, for while this Dracula is literally a 'blood-sucker', it becomes clear that Chris Bond is also using the term to say something about certain echelons of society!

This is what he says about his play:

Passion and fun are what I like best in the theatre: music, sex, violence, wild words and cheap laughs. My play needs a performance style that's big and bold, but it has to be based on emotional truth. I write about people who are driven by obsession because they make good drama. All of the characters in The Blood of Dracula are obsessed: Jonathan Harker with consummating his marriage; Sir Robert Seward with his sausages and his guilt; Dr Tanya Van Helsing with her work; the Crebbs family with the danger of their situation; and Count Dracula with what Count Dracula is always obsessed with. When in doubt look for obsession, and the jokes will look after themselves!

THE BLOOD OF DRACULA

C A S T L I S T

Jonathan Harker	An Englishman (possibly a bit repressed)
Lucie Harker	His wife
Sir Robert Seward	Her father, a manufacturer of quality meat products and self-made millionaire
Dr Tanya Van Helsing	An eminent scientist from the University of Vienna
Mr and Mrs Crebbs	Servants to Count Dracula; they might look remarkably alike
Count Dracula	A vampire

The first production of this play, in a slightly extended version called simply *Dracula*, was performed at the Little Theatre, Bristol, in February 1981. The cast included Albie Woodington, Ishia Bennison, Nigel Cooke, Rosalind March, Stuart Cox and Daniel Day-Lewis.

The play was directed by George Costigan and designed by Bob Crowley.

ACT ONE

The drawing room of the lodge of Castle Dracula, Transylvania. It is a night in June in the year 1880.

*The lodge has recently been converted into a bijou holiday dwelling, including the installation of a handsome set of French windows up centre. To one side of them there is a writing desk and chair and in front of them a couch on which **Lucie Harker** lies, apparently asleep. She is very pale and has a silk scarf tied around her neck. A tin trunk stands on the floor at the end of the couch. On the other side of the room **Jonathan Harker** leans against a massive fireplace gloomily drinking a whisky and soda. Hanging down next to the fireplace there is a bell rope and beside that a door to the rest of the lodge.*

__Harker__ sniffs: doesn't like what he can smell. Sniffs again. Checks his armpits. Not them. Sniffs again, then sniffs his way over to the tin trunk. Checks the doors and tentatively opens the trunk.

HARKER   Oh, really…!

Removes a string of sausages from the trunk with extreme distaste. A wolf howls sexily outside the French windows.

And you can shut up as well!

Drops sausages back in the trunk and slams lid. Snatches a holiday brochure circa 1880 from the end of the couch.

(*Reading.*) 'Thomas Cook & Sons are proud and privileged to announce to their patrons a new range of holidays for the discerning traveller during this year of grace eighteen hundred and eighty.' Ha! 'We have recently become the sole agents for a few selected bijou holiday residences in lovely unspoilt Transylvania. Peace, quiet and tranquillity amidst the flora and fauna of a land that time forgot.' Ha! 'May we suggest that this is the ideal holiday for your honeymoon?' Ha! 'Why not while away those special hours in a fully modernised and gaslit lodge of an ancient landmark like, for instance, Castle Dracula.'

Thunder, lights flicker.

Ha! Peace, quiet, tranquillity and a permanent Force 9 thunderstorm to feast your earholes on.

Wolves howl.

Not to mention the flora and flaming fauna!

Harker *rushes to the writing desk, grabs a pistol from the desk drawer and opens the French windows. They open inwards and a howling gale nearly blows him into the audience. He claws his way back across the carpet and fires into the garden.*

We're on our honeymoon dammit! (*Bang.*) And we don't want to hear your bally moanings and groanings all night: (*Bang.*) it'll put us right orf! (*Bang.*) If we ever get round to it. (*Bang.*) So let's have a bit of peace and tranquillity (*Bang.*) you overgrown doormats. (*Bang.*)

Lucie *rises from the sofa, apparently sleepwalking, and heads for the French windows.* **Harker** *shuts them with difficulty. He turns back to the room and sees her.*

Lucie! Darling! You're up! Um... better now hm? Ready for bed, hm? Shall I get the maid to help you undress, or shall I help myself? Help you myself I mean?

Lucie *sighs loudly and longingly, turns and goes back to the sofa. Lies down and appears to go back to sleep.*

Oh dammit all Lucie! There's nothing the matter with you woman!

Snatches up brochure again.

'May we suggest that this is the ideal holiday for your honeymoon?' No you may not. Not when the bride gets the vapours the minute she toddles over the threshold. Stop it! Control yourself man, ring for the butler chappie and have another drink.

Pulls on bell rope. It comes away in his hand and showers him with dust.

Damn and blast it woman, now look what you've made me do! Can't you see what you're doing to me. Lying there, looking so pale, and so helpless, and so – stop it! Stop it Jonathan! What would Nanny say if she heard you behaving like this? Eh? 'Stop it,' she'd say.

Crebbs *enters behind him and watches. He wears a large string of garlic around his neck.*

(*Smacking himself on the wrist.*) Stop it, stop it, stop it.

CREBBS   You ring mein Herr?

HARKER   Ha! What? No. Yes. Ah. Crebbs. Yuk, have you been eating raw garlic again Crebbs?

CREBBS   Yes mein Herr.

HARKER   How many times have I told you, Crebbs, you must not eat raw garlic?

CREBBS   Nein... Nein...

HARKER   At least nine, and we've only been here two days.

CREBBS   Pardon, mein Herr?

HARKER   What?

CREBBS   Pardon, mein Herr?

HARKER	Eh? Yes, I s'pose so, it doesn't look any worse than the rest of you. Just stop eating raw garlic will you?
CREBBS	But I find it help, mein Herr.
HARKER	What, you mean it helps it grow? Keeps it healthy?
CREBBS	Keeps what healthy, mein Herr?
HARKER	Yes.
CREBBS	Mein Herr?
HARKER	Yes! That long thin stuff sprouting out the top of where your head would be if the good Lord hadn't given you a turnip instead.
CREBBS	I not understand. What you want mein Herr?
HARKER	No, I certainly do not want your hair; I've got a perfectly good headful of my own. Look, double handfuls of the stuff, and all good British fields of waving wheat colour.
CREBBS	Ah! You mean mine hair mein Herr! Mine hair!
HARKER	Oh just shut up about your hair. And no more eating raw garlic, Crebbs.
CREBBS	But it keep me safe.
HARKER	What are you talking about? Keeps off the sneezles, that sort of thing?
CREBBS	(*Meaningfully.*) It stop me getting sore throat sir.
HARKER	Really. Well, it's dashed antisocial Crebbs, so stop it.
CREBBS	(*Offering garlic.*) You have clove please?
HARKER	Certainly not, I can't stand the stuff. Besides, Mrs Harker will be waking up again soon and she's not going to want me breathing garlic all over her while we're… stop it Johnny, stop it!

Harker turns away and walks rapidly round the

room smacking himself.

*Music as **Crebbs** approaches **Lucie** holding the garlic in front of him. She moans as he gets close to the sofa. He bends over and breathes garlic into her face. She groans and writhes. **Harker** turns.*

What the...! How dare you, I'll have you horsewhipped you damned...

***Crebbs** legs it round the sofa and opens the French windows. There is a howling gale. **Crebbs** and **Harker** are blown back and then **Crebbs** struggles out into the garden pursued by **Harker**. The music grows louder and a throbbing heartbeat can be heard on top. Lights flicker and dim. A wolf howls very close outside. Its eyes glow in the garden.*

LUCIE   (*Trancelike.*) Yes, I hear you.

She stands.

Yes, I must come when you call.

She goes to the French windows. The wolf goes bananas.

(*Different voice.*) No... please no...

*She struggles against the invisible force that is pulling her into the garden, clings to the window frame. Just when she can't hold out any longer, the door to the drawing room opens and **Sir Robert Seward** pokes his head into the room.*

SEWARD   Hey up, where's my pussycat?

*An enormous thunderclap. Lights flicker. **Lucie** screams and falls. The wolf's eyes go out. Music and heartbeat stop. Lights return to normal. Wind continues.*

Well, I'll go to the foot of the stairs.

***Seward** rushes across to **Lucie**. **Dr Tanya Van Helsing** enters behind him carrying a large doctor's* *bag and a box containing her blood 'transfer' equipment.*

What's that Harker lad of thine a-thinking of?

Seward and *Van Helsing* battle against the wind to carry *Lucie* back to the sofa.

This is her, Dr Van Helsing, this is my daughter.

VAN HELSING   If you wouldn't mind closing the windows, Sir Robert?

SEWARD   Oh aye. Reet.

*He goes to do so and meets **Harker** coming back in.*

Van Helsing begins to give *Lucie* an incredibly thorough medical examination which includes taking samples of skin tissue, blood, saliva, etc. and making up slides and examining them under a microscope.

HARKER   Sir Robert, thank God you're back.

SEWARD   Where've you been lad? Ring for that Crebbs feller and get our Lucie some brandy.

HARKER   Ha! I'll ring that Crebbs feller's neck when I get hold of him. And anyway, the bell's jiggered.

SEWARD   Reet. I'll fetch it mesen then.

Seward exits.

HARKER   (*Calls after him.*) What about the Doctor – couldn't you find one?

*But **Seward** has gone.*

(*To **Van Helsing**.*) Did you bring a quack with you?

VAN HELSING   A quack?

HARKER   Yes, Sir Robert had some notion that Lucie was a bit under the weather so he toddled off to get the doc.

VAN HELSING   Ah, a doctor. Allow me to introduce myself: Dr Tanya Van Helsing of the University of Vienna.

HARKER   Oh, you're the quack. Frightfully sorry old chap, Johnny Harker, though between you and me I think you're wasting your time. Just a fit of the vapours, y'know, young woman, too much excitement, laced herself up a bit tight, just got hitched, great expectations and all that, 'spect you see quite a lot of it in your line eh?

VAN HELSING   I dare say.

*She continues concentrating on examining **Lucie**.*

HARKER   Er... Do you mind if I ask you something doctor?

VAN HELSING   Please do.

HARKER   Well, I don't want to be rude, but... why are you wearing women's clothes?

VAN HELSING   I beg your pardon?

HARKER   Why are you dressed up as a woman?

VAN HELSING   Possibly because I am a woman.

HARKER   Good God. So you are. Apparently, well, obviously, I mean you've even got the bits at the front.

VAN HELSING   Indeed. And now if you'll excuse me I must attend to my patient.

Seward *re-enters with a brandy decanter and a glass.*

SEWARD   Here you go doctor...

VAN HELSING   No, thank you, Sir Robert, a stimulant would not be advisable at the present moment.

SEWARD   Oh reet. I'll drink it mesen then.

HARKER   Over here, Sir Robert...

Harker *takes **Seward** off into a corner.*

Look, I don't want to worry you sir, but this doctor chappie, well, he isn't one.

SEWARD   I'nt a Doctor?

HARKER   Well, I dunno about that, but he certainly isn't a chappie.

SEWARD   Harker, she is a doctor, she is probably t'most brilliant medical practitioner in the whole of Europe. So calm down lad, I know things haven't worked out too rosy so far, and I'm sorry...

HARKER   (*Interrupting.*) I should think you jolly are, Transylvania! I never liked the idea in the first place. What was wrong with Weston-Super-Mare that's what I'd like to know? Lucie was all for Weston too, but no, you had to get a letter from this bally Count Dracula...

Thunder. Lights flicker.

...about his bally bijou holiday residence and that's it, it had to be Transylballyvania for the honeymoon didn't it?

SEWARD   I just wanted Lucie to have t'best.

HARKER   Ha!

SEWARD   Summat a bit different...

HARKER   Ha!

SEWARD   Summat romantic...

HARKER   Ha!

SEWARD   Summat out the way where you could be alone together. Just t'two of you.

HARKER   Three of us.

SEWARD   Eh?

HARKER   Well, there's you as well isn't there?

SEWARD   Aye but... well, I'm very fond of yon pussycat y'know.

HARKER   I dare say. But that isn't why you came.

SEWARD   I'nt it?

HARKER   No. It's bally sausages again isn't it?

SEWARD   What dost t'mean lad?

HARKER   Ha! Don't think you can pull the wool over mine Sir Robert. I know what you've got in that tin trunk of ours.

Seward instinctively looks towards it.

Go on, open it, and I'll lay you twenty guineas to a brass farthing it's full to the scuppers with Seward and Browne's Original Recipe Finest Pork Sausages. Well?

SEWARD   Well – your German person is very partial to a bit of sausage, and I thought maybe...

HARKER   God's teeth man, don't you ever think of anything else? You must be damn near a millionaire, you must be, and yet you spend half your life up to your armpits in offal 'cos you won't let anyone else know your precious recipe, and now here you are traipsing along on your daughter's honeymoon with a trunk full of the wretched things.

SEWARD   (*Furious.*) Take care son Harker, there's nowt wretched about them sausages, and there i'nt no offal in 'em either. The Seward & Browne Sausage is a Quality Pork Product made to an original recipe, which as you rightly say is known only to myself. It's my life's work that sausage, and it is eaten and enjoyed at every aristocratic dining table in England, including royalty! Aye, it has made me a bit o'brass, and doubtless one day it'll make yon lass o' mine a very rich pussycat – providing I'm satisfied that she, and them as is closest to her, will treat it with t'respect it deserves.

HARKER   Oh. I see. Yes, Sir Robert.

SEWARD   So let's hear no more about it.

HARKER	No, Sir Robert. Sorry, Sir Robert.

Van Helsing completes her examination of Lucie and now unlocks her blood 'transfer' box.

SEWARD	Reet. Now then, doctor, what's to do?
VAN HELSING	Your daughter is in perfect health, Sir Robert – except in one respect. She is suffering from acute anaemia.
SEWARD	Ee, what's that?
VAN HELSING	Under normal circumstances anaemia is a deficiency of red corpuscles in the blood...

Wolf howls outside. They all turn and listen.

...but microscopic analysis shows that is not the problem in your daughter's case. She is simply suffering from a lack of blood.

Wolf howls again. They all turn and listen.

HARKER	How very unpleasant, do we have to listen to this?
SEWARD	Well, what ar't going to do about it?
VAN HELSING	Give her some of Mr Harker's.
HARKER	What!
VAN HELSING	Yes, don't be alarmed Mr Harker, in theory a blood transfer, or 'transfusion' is a perfectly minor operation. And it is also extremely exciting as this will be the first blood 'transfusion' to be attempted between two living human beings. You are fortunate that I have been hoping for such an opportunity for some time and have therefore been carrying the requisite equipment round with me.

She has now set up the equipment.

Now what happens is this. I merely make a small incision in your arm...

HARKER	Merely?

VAN HELSING	Yes. And open a small vein.
HARKER	Oh a small one, that's good. Why not try the jolly old jugular? (*Aside to **Sir Robert**.*) The woman's cracked.
VAN HELSING	The blood…

Wolf howls outside. They all turn to listen.

The blood…

Wolf howls again. They all turn to listen.

It…

They all turn to listen. Silence.

Interesting. It is then pumped along this tube here and into your wife's arm by means of another small incision.

SEWARD	I see. Sounds simple enough.
VAN HELSING	Yes. So Mr Harker, if you would roll up your sleeve…?
HARKER	You don't seriously think I'm going to let you start cutting lumps out of me do you?
VAN HELSING	Yes, Mr Harker. I imagine that you would wish to assist your wife in any way you can.
HARKER	Well, you imagine wrong, we're not Red Indians y'know. I married the girl because I wanted a wife, not a blood brother.
VAN HELSING	It is precisely because you married her that I mistakenly supposed that you would be the one most anxious to assist her, however…
SEWARD	(*Taking off his jacket and rolling up his sleeve.*) Oh come on the pair of you. Get on with it lass, you can use my arm if it'll suit.
VAN HELSING	Thank you Sir Robert.

*She attaches one tube to **Sir Robert's** arm and the other to **Lucie's** during this next.*

HARKER   And what do you know about marriage, Mrs Clever Clogs? I see you're not wearing a ring, so some poor devil's been spared a terminal dose of earache.

VAN HELSING   It is true I have no direct experience of marriage in the clinical sense, but I have observed that it appears to draw the participants into a close emotional dependency. Are you quite comfortable Sir Robert?

SEWARD   Aye.

VAN HELSING   Good, then I would be grateful if you would answer a few questions Mr Harker.

HARKER   Ha!

VAN HELSING   Are you a particularly passionate man, Mr Harker?

HARKER   Of course I'm not. I'm English dammit. That's to say, of course I'm passionate, but I don't get steamed up about it.

VAN HELSING   I see. And what about your wife's neck?

HARKER   What about it?

VAN HELSING   What do you... think about it?

HARKER   Eh? Well, it seems to keep her head on all right.

SEWARD   Is there summat up with Lucie's neck?

VAN HELSING   Keep still Sir Robert. Look – here.

*She removes the scarf from round **Lucie's** neck. There are two large punctures in the skin.*

SEWARD   Hecky thump!

VAN HELSING   Keep still.

HARKER   Yuk, looks as if she's been sticking herself with a hatpin.

VAN HELSING	Is your wife in the habit of sticking hatpins into herself Mr Harker?
HARKER	How should I know? I mean she never used to flake out on me before we got married.
SEWARD	Warrisit doctor? Insect bites?
VAN HELSING	Perhaps. I think that will do Sir Robert.

Removes tubes and dismantles apparatus and puts it away.

HARKER	Insects now! Place is a health hazard as well. Ha! But I'm not surprised, not with that cess pit up the road – Castle Dracula.

Thunder. Lights flicker. **Lucie** *moans and stirs.*

VAN HELSING	Excellent, she's coming round.
LUCIE	What's happening? Where am I?
VAN HELSING	You've been unwell Mrs Harker, but don't worry, I'm a doctor.
HARKER	Yes, and I'm a husband, so would you excuse us please?
LUCIE	Cold, I feel so cold.
VAN HELSING	Your hands?

Van Helsing *rubs* ***Lucie's*** *hands.*

HARKER	I'll do that if you don't mind...
LUCIE	No. Here... (*She touches her neck.*) He's gone... Where is he? He was so soft, so smooth, so silky...
VAN HELSING	Who has gone, Mrs Harker?
HARKER	No, I'm here old girl, let me kiss it better...
LUCIE	No, you're not the one! He wasn't clumsy, he wasn't rough like you.
HARKER	Well, you try shaving in cold water, woman.

VAN HELSING   Quiet. Mrs Harker, I want you to tell me when you first felt this coldness. Will you begin please.

LUCIE   Yes. It was evening. Yesterday morning I suppose. And Daddy and Johnny had gone for a walk. Up to – that place.

VAN HELSING   To the castle?

LUCIE   Yes. I think Daddy wanted to give the Count some of his sausages.

VAN HELSING   Count Dracula?

Thunder. Followed by a continuous heartbeat.

SEWARD   What's that noise?

HARKER   Probably the plumbing, whole place is falling to bits.

VAN HELSING   And what did you do while they were out, Mrs Harker?

LUCIE   I wrote a letter. To my Aunt Mary.

HARKER   Is she the one who sent us that hideous toast rack?

VAN HELSING   Please, Mr Harker...

HARKER   Miserable old bat.

LUCIE   Ah! No! Is it there again?

VAN HELSING   Sir Robert, if you wish me to help your daughter would you please ask Mr Harker to be silent.

SEWARD   Shut th'trap lad.

HARKER   I... Yes sir.

VAN HELSING   You were writing to your Aunt Mary, Mrs Harker...?

LUCIE   Yes. And I heard something. Behind me. As if something was... beating against the glass. Trying to get into the room...

VAN HELSING   A bird?

LUCIE	Yes. I don't know. Like a bird. And I went to look… To see what it was.
VAN HELSING	And what was it?
LUCIE	I don't know. I couldn't see. So I…

Heartbeat increases. **Lucie** *gasps for breath.*

I… I put my hand out and… and then…

Wolf howls outside. Thunder. Lights flicker. **Lucie** *faints.*

HARKER	Oh Lord, here we go again. Roll up, roll up, see the incredible fainting woman, she's up, she's down, she's on the ground.
SEWARD	Control thesen Harker. Pull th'self together lad.
VAN HELSING	And when you returned from your walk you found her like this?
SEWARD	Aye. Thought she were having forty winks.
VAN HELSING	And there was nothing disturbed in the room.
SEWARD	Nay, I don't think so. Mrs Crebbs were in here, dusting like.
VAN HELSING	Mrs Crebbs?
HARKER	Wife of the abominable Crebbs, he of the garlic breath and roving hands.
VAN HELSING	I'd like to talk to her.
SEWARD	Reet. I'll go fetch her.

Seward *exits.*

VAN HELSING	Was your wife wearing this scarf when you went for your walk Mr Harker?
HARKER	Dunno. Don't think so.
VAN HELSING	But when you returned, was she wearing the scarf then?

HARKER   Um... Yes, I think she was. But what's so...

*Seward returns with **Mrs Crebbs** who wears heads of garlic as drop earrings and a necklace.*

Did you know your husband was a sex maniac, Mrs Crebbs?

MRS CREBBS   What do you mean mein Herr?

HARKER   Now don't start that again.

VAN HELSING   You were dusting in here the evening Mrs Harker fell ill Mrs Crebbs?

MRS CREBBS   Yes, doctor.

VAN HELSING   Was there anyone, or anything in here with her?

MRS CREBBS   Any thing, doctor?

VAN HELSING   Yes, a bird perhaps.

MRS CREBBS   I not see any bird, doctor.

VAN HELSING   A cat then?

MRS CREBBS   What you say, doctor?

VAN HELSING   A cat.

SEWARD   A cat? What's cat got to do with...?

VAN HELSING   'Something smooth,' she said, Sir Robert, 'Something silky.'

HARKER   Ha! See any koala bears wandering about Mrs Crebbs? Any mongooses? A couple of ring-tailed lemurs swinging from the picture rails perhaps?

VAN HELSING   Was there a cat in here Mrs Crebbs?

MRS CREBBS   If there is cat I not see him doctor.

VAN HELSING   All right, Mrs Crebbs, that will be all thank you.

Mrs Crebbs curtsies and makes for the door.

Why did you put the scarf round her neck Mrs Crebbs?

MRS CREBBS   She breathing… (*Realises her mistake and turns slowly.*) She breathing heavy. And I think she is maybe get sore throat doctor.

VAN HELSING   Did you now. So Mrs Harker was sitting here wasn't she, Mrs Crebbs?

Van Helsing sits at the desk. Heartbeat returns.

And she heard a noise didn't she, Mrs Crebbs? Behind her. Did you hear it too, Mrs Crebbs?

MRS CREBBS   I not remember, doctor.

VAN HELSING   Then let me refresh your memory; she heard a sound as if something was beating against the glass, as if something was trying to get into the room…

MRS CREBBS   You are stopping this, doctor.

VAN HELSING   And Mrs Harker thought it was a bird didn't she?

MRS CREBBS   I…

VAN HELSING   And she went to look…

MRS CREBBS   Doctor, you not know what you are…

VAN HELSING   To look out of the French windows…

MRS CREBBS   Doctor…

Mrs Crebbs begins to mutter a prayer and count her garlic necklace as if it were a rosary.

VAN HELSING   And what happened next Mrs Crebbs?

*Heartbeat increases. **Mrs Crebbs** counts faster.*

I think she opened the French windows, Mrs Crebbs. Like this.

*Van Helsing opens the French windows. Howling wind. There is thunder, and an enormous bat flies into the room and disappears into the fireplace and up the chimney. **Mrs Crebbs** screams. **Harker** hides. **Lucie** wakes and makes for the French windows. **Van***

*Helsing restrains her with difficulty. **Seward** grabs a shotgun from an umbrella stand by the door and empties both barrels up the chimney. Half a ton of soot falls on his head and hundreds of bats fly out of the chimney and fly wildly round the room screaming their heads off and getting in everyone's hair. The lights flicker continuously. Eventually the bats fly out of the French windows and everything returns to normal.*

***Mrs Crebbs** has vanished. **Sir Robert** is holding an ancient and soot-stained piece of parchment that has come down the chimney.*

LUCIE He's gone! Where is he?

*A final thunderclap, and **Lucie** faints again.*

VAN HELSING Where's Mrs Crebbs.

SEWARD Where's Harker?

HARKER (*Emerging from behind sofa.*) Where's Nanny?

VAN HELSING Help me back to the couch with her, Sir Robert.

HARKER Never mind about her, what about me! What about little Johnny? I want to lie on the sofa! It's my turn! She's always lying on the sofa!

*He giggles and repeats, 'Me, me, me' and 'My turn' and 'Johnny's a good boy, Johnny's turn' etc in a feverish mutter, until **Van Helsing** slaps his face exceedingly hard.*

You hit me.

VAN HELSING Yes, Mr Harker, you had become hysterical, now why don't you go and get drunk, or wax your moustache, or do any of the thousand and one things an irritating young man might do instead of showing off in front of people who have more important matters to consider.

HARKER You hit me.

VAN HELSING　And I will do so again if I consider it necessary.

HARKER　All right, all right, 'nuff said.

*He backs off to the brandy decanter that **Seward** brought in and settles down to some serious drinking.*

VAN HELSING　Now, Sir Robert, what have you got there?

SEWARD　I dunno. It come down t'chimney with all them screaming little horrors. Burrit looks like double Dutch to me.

***Van Helsing** takes parchment.*

VAN HELSING　Hm. It appears to be written in some early dialect form of Slavonic. Time has not dealt kindly with the… ink, but it would seem to be some form of testament…

Music.

(*Reading, translating as she goes.*) 'Given under the hand of I, Johannes Brucke the younger, master carpenter of Bistritz on this day I calculate to be the 20th August in the year of our sweet Lord Jesu seventeen hundred and twelve. I write these words in an extremity of terror, and indeed, I think my mind so mixed' – no, 'disordered' is better, – 'I think my mind so disordered that were it not for the evidence – the foul evidence, upon my own body and the bodies of my once dear companions, of the truth of what I thus write, I doubt not but I would declare myself to be quite mad. I do not know when the Ochtsturn…'

SEWARD　T'what?

VAN HELSING　'Ochsturn', not a word I am familiar with, but the syllabic translation would be 'undead'.

SEWARD　Undead?

VAN HELSING　Yes. (*Continues reading.*) 'I do not know when the thing, the Undead, will return. Or in what shape, since it is sometime a wolf, and at other a great vershtun...'

SEWARD   Vershtun?

VAN HELSING   'Vershtun' is the Slavonic word for a bat, Sir Robert.

SEWARD   A bat? But great heavens...!

Seward rushes to the French windows and looks out.

You don't think...?

VAN HELSING   I have not sufficient information to form a worthwhile opinion as yet Sir Robert. Shall I continue?

SEWARD   Aye lass.

VAN HELSING   'And at other a great bat, but more terrible still than all these it appear in that familiar shape God first made Adam in, my own. So I will set down all in haste that may be some assistance to any so cursed with ill fortune as to come after me to this place. It cast no shadow on the sweet earth, nor yet its image will not stain a glass.' Mirror? Yes, 'Its image will not stain a mirror. It fear the godly sun above all things and only prey in hours of dark. It may not come near the poor wild garlic flower. A cross – a crucifix – will hold it off and burn it while the hand be strong that hold it. It will not eat nor drink of any natural food as common creatures all will do, but ever seek its succour only in blood of human souls. If...' Here it is blotted. 'It comes... I cannot...'

Music finishes.

SEWARD   Cannot what?

VAN HELSING   That is all. There it breaks off.

SEWARD   But what do you make of it?

VAN HELSING   The paper is certainly old, and although calligraphy is no more than a hobby with me, the handwriting seems to be consistent with the author being in a state of extreme nervous tension.

HARKER   Ha! That's it! Stop there. You're not suggesting that we take these ravings seriously are you? Oh come on Sir Robert, you don't believe this rubbish surely?

SEWARD   (*Who appears to have aged twenty years in the last five minutes.*) I don't know any more lad. I don't know.

HARKER   But it's the work of a madman or... or a practical joke or some such nonsense.

VAN HELSING   A painful joke for the author I suspect.

SEWARD   What does th'mean?

VAN HELSING   Well, I cannot be certain without the benefit of chemical analysis of course, but this document looks to me as if it was written in blood.

*Wolf howls. **Lucie** opens her eyes.*

SEWARD   Blood?

*Wolf howls. **Lucie** sniffs.*

VAN HELSING   Yes. Though I doubt whether after this lapse of time even laboratory conditions could determine whether it was animal or human blood.

*Wolf howls. **Lucie** has risen to her feet and now utters a piercing scream and hurls herself at **Van Helsing**, tears the parchment from her hand and starts eating it. **Van Helsing** and **Seward** try to restrain her. They force her back onto the couch.*

VAN HELSING   Hold her! Hold her!

*She hastily prepares a large hypodermic syringe and gives **Lucie** a shot. She quietens.*

SEWARD   In God's name Van Helsing, does th'know what's wrong with her?

VAN HELSING No, I don't know, Sir Robert.

Takes a half-chewed scrap of parchment from **Lucie's** *mouth.*

Or perhaps I am afraid to know.

SEWARD Speak plain woman, what does th' think?

VAN HELSING Very well Sir Robert, fantastical as it may sound I believe your daughter to be at least partly in the grip of something unnatural. Something 'undead', which has been feeding upon her blood and in so doing has contaminated her soul.

SEWARD No, please – no! not her blood.

VAN HELSING I understand your revulsion Sir Robert, but the proposition is not so absurd as it may at first appear. Since the dawn of civilisation human beings have believed in the rejuvenative powers of blood and drunk it accordingly. The ancient cultures of Egypt, Assyria, Palestine, China and Peru have all indulged in it, and in Tibetan Lamaism an entire group of gods are portrayed with dripping fangs. Perhaps these primitive peoples made the assumption that since when the blood flowed out of a wounded animal or man, the life ebbed out as well, blood must be the source of life, and therefore drank it to make themselves stronger.

SEWARD But this is a bat we're talking about, woman, not a God!

VAN HELSING Yes, Sir Robert, and here perhaps zoology may assist us for in the Pampas region of South America there exists a small bat no larger than a kitten which is parasitic upon the local cattle. It feeds exclusively upon their blood, and it is called a vampire.

Thunder. Music. Wolf howls. The French windows fly open. **Dracula** *stands framed in the doorway.*

VAN HELSING   And who the devil are you?

DRACULA   I am Dracula. Count Dracula. Good evening. Sir Robert. Mr Harker. And the young lady upon the couch must be your new bride Mrs...ss...ss... (*He appears to have difficulty in stopping himself from hissing.*) ...Harker. Is she unwell?

VAN HELSING   Why do you ask that?

DRACULA   She has something of a grave look. These two gentlemen I had the pleasure of meeting last night when Sir Robert brought me some of his excellent ss...ss...sausages, but you Madame are unknown to me.

VAN HELSING   Dr Tanya Van Helsing of the University of Vienna.

DRACULA   An unexpected pleasure, but no less delightful for that I do assure you...

He kisses her hand and lingers over it. She tries to pull away but he keeps hold of her hand.

Forgive me, but that is a most charming brooch upon your throat. (***Van Helsing*** *is wearing a choker.*) May I?

VAN HELSING   I...

Dracula *tilts up her chin and bends to examine the brooch. Exhales loudly, somewhere between a snarl and a sigh.* ***Van Helsing*** *pulls away.*

DRACULA   Your pardon, but one seldom sees a sight so fine.

VAN HELSING   As this brooch?

DRACULA   Of course, though if the jewel be fine it needs as fine a setting. Perhaps you will allow me time to study them both at some more convenient time?

VAN HELSING   Perhaps.

DRACULA   I shall look forward to that time with a relish as keen as a connoisseur awaiting the tasting of a new wine. You shall not deny me doctor, I shall insist.

HARKER   (*Emerging from a drunken stupor.*) Wine? D'you say you had some wine old chap?

DRACULA   No, Mr Harker, I never drink wine, but perhaps I might taste another of your excellent sausages Sir Robert. I find I have developed a taste for them.

HARKER   (*Lurching over to the tin trunk.*) Yes, course you can old chap, got a whole bally tin trunk full of the beggars here.

Harker tosses a sausage to **Dracula**.

Here you are, Dracula old son, get your gnashers round that.

DRACULA   (*Raises sausage.*) Your health Sir Robert. Doctor.

He fangs the sausage. Wolf howls outside.

Ah, listen to them, the children of the night. What music they make.

HARKER   Music?

DRACULA   Oh Mr Harker, you city dwellers cannot understand, but you are in Transylvania now, and Transylvania is not England. Our ways are not your ways, nor our history and traditions your history and traditions. We are no island race, protected from invasion by the sea, and yet we are as proud as you and with some cause. For here, amidst the very whirlpool of the European races we have fought against Bulgar, Saxon, Turk, Wallachian, Magyar, Lombard and the Hun, until there cannot be a yard of soil in all this land unmoistened by the blood of valiant men. Our sheep and cattle graze upon the grass that grows from it, our trees are rooted in its ruddy depth and suck their life and health from out of it.

Wolf howls grow louder outside.

And perhaps the children of our nights can scent its sweetness in our very air and sing their praises to it. But listen carefully and you will hear the descant to their song, sung by the counter-tenor of the night, the bat!

Dracula flings open the French windows.

Come, doctor, will you not walk with me on such a night as this? I can assure you that no living thing will harm you whilst you are upon my arm.

VAN HELSING I cannot pretend that your offer does not tempt me, Count.

SEWARD Doctor?

VAN HELSING Yes, Sir Robert, I am a doctor, but I am also a woman, as the Count is well aware. (*She takes a mirror from her bag and adjusts a couple of curls.*) And perhaps in all my studies I have neglected a part of myself that is as precious to me as knowledge. Your arm, Count.

SEWARD No, doctor, no!

VAN HELSING One question before we go, Count.

DRACULA Your servant.

VAN HELSING (*Holding mirror in front of his face.*) Why is there no reflection of you in this mirror?

Dracula snarls horribly, raises his arms, his cloak spread out. Thunder. Lights flicker. Mirror shatters. Blackout. Howling wind.

Lights up. Dracula has been replaced by the huge bat which now flies out of the French windows and away.

VAN HELSING After it!

SEWARD Reet!

Seward grabs shotgun. He and Van Helsing pursue bat out of the French windows. Harker and Lucie are left alone. Music.

VAN HELSING   (*Off.*) There! There!

HARKER   What's she rabbiting on about now? Women, always bossing you about…

SEWARD   (*Off.*) There! Round the front…

HARKER   And nagging on at you and going bonkers and fainting and not giving you your oats. Ha!

Shotgun is fired off.

'Cept for Nanny of course. Good old Nanny. Wish I'd married Nanny instead of you, you washed out old ratbag.

Thunder. Lights flicker. **Dracula** *stands in the doorway.*

DRACULA   (*Exhales.*)

HARKER   Have you caught a chill old chap?

DRACULA   (*Exhales.*)

HARKER   I should get the quack to have a look at that, sounds nasty.

DRACULA   (*Exhales.*)

HARKER   Very nasty in fact.

DRACULA   (*Exhales.*)

HARKER   Er… was there anything in particular?

DRACULA   I want your wife.

HARKER   Yes, well she's asleep at the moment, as per usual.

DRACULA   No. The one you love is mine already. I have known her. Already my mark is on her throat. Flesh of my flesh, blood of my blood. I have come to claim her.

HARKER   What?

DRACULA   (*Howls like a wolf.*)

HARKER   Oh my God, you're... Nanny?

Harker faints.

DRACULA   Come!

Lucie stirs and moans.

DRACULA   Come!

Lucie whimpers and rises to her feet.

DRACULA   Come!

LUCIE   No... No...

Lucie walks to him. Stops.

DRACULA   Your ss...scarf.

LUCIE   No... No...

But she takes it off as if in a trance. **Dracula** *exhales deeply, howls again and then plunges his teeth into her neck. He drinks noisily, then scoops her up and stands framed in the French windows with blood running from her neck and down his chin.*

SEWARD   (*Off. Coming to the door.*) Ee, I could've sworn I hit it.

Dracula laughs.

VAN HELSING   (*Off.*) Yes. Strange.

Dracula laughs.

VAN HELSING   (*Off.*) What was that?

*Dracula laughs. **Van Helsing** and **Seward** burst in.*

SEWARD   No! Lucie!

Dracula laughs.

Blackout.

END OF ACT ONE

ACT TWO

A BURIAL VAULT BELOW CASTLE DRACULA.

*Stairs lead down into it from the castle courtyard.
There are arches leading off to other burial chambers,
and several decayed stone tombs with lids on.*

Water drips. A wolf howls in the distance.

Crebbs *enters from another burial chamber, pushing
a wheelbarrow full of earth with a spade and a rake
on top of it. He still wears his garlic and also carries a
lantern and a bucket of water.*

CREBBS   Work, work, work. Will it never cease?

*He drops the wheelbarrow by the largest tomb and
begins to heave off the lid.*

Why we can't change to wooden coffins I don't
know. Is OK for undead; if you have strength of
twenty is simple. Is sun go down, wolf call, lift lid,
is simple, but for ordinary Christian soul is damn
backbreaking work.

Gets lid off.

CREBBS   These vampires is all the same, never thinking of no
one but themselves.

Lucie *sits bolt upright in the tomb.*

CREBBS   What you do there? Is Dracula bed.

LUCIE   The Count said I might rest here.

CREBBS   You should be 'shamed of yourself. Young girl, just
married and… well, I s'pose is not your fault. But
you get out please. Out! Out!

Lucie *gets out of tomb.*

CREBBS   Is not allowed to sleep during night, is only
sleeping during day. How else I clean and tidy?

He begins to shovel earth out of the wheelbarrow into tomb, and sprinkle it with water from bucket.

CREBBS Though why he can't make his own bed sometime I not know.

Lucie thoughtfully pulls a long worm out of the earth in the wheelbarrow. Holds it up and then puts one end in her mouth and sucks it up like a strand of spaghetti. Crebbs sees it disappear.

CREBBS No, dirty. Is not good. Spit him out. Is make you sick. You are only feeding from human person now or is bad news for tum-tum, ja?

Lucie delicately removes worm from her mouth and replaces it in wheelbarrow.

CREBBS Is good girl. You have much to learn ja? You not worry, soon grow big teeth, learn flying, all sorts.

LUCIE But I'm thirsty.

CREBBS Well why not popping over to village and wait till pubs are chucking out? Is good for practice on drunkens, they not run so fast.

LUCIE I'd much rather stay with you, Crebbs.

CREBBS Is good. I teach much. You good girl, I do your bed next.

He pauses for breath, panting. Loosens his collar. Lucie watches with interest.

That better. Count he like me dressed proper alltimes, but you not tell, ja?

LUCIE Oh no, Crebbs, I won't tell him.

CREBBS Is good. You are scratching my back and I will be scratching yours, ja?

LUCIE Oh yes please.

CREBBS Is good for have company to talk to 'stead of Mrs Crebbs go on and on nag nag nag. 'This not right for us, Jacov, we go Hell for it. Is not good work for us.' She think job grow on trees nowdays? Her think I like do this? Her think I like work for Dracula for lousy money and bedboard? But maybe she right, maybe we quit soon.

LUCIE   Yes, Crebbs, you work so hard, and you look so hot and tired. Why don't you have a rest?

CREBBS   Is not possible.

LUCIE   Well, at least take off your garlic. It looks so heavy round your poor neck.

CREBBS   Ja, is heavy.

LUCIE   And it keeps getting in your way.

CREBBS   Ja, is nuisance.

LUCIE   Well, why don't you slip it off, I'm sure you'd feel much cooler.

CREBBS   Ja, is right.

Crebbs dumps spade and begins to take off garlic.

LUCIE   (*Exhales.*)

Crebbs whips round and replaces garlic.

CREBBS   So! Is please not try it on Missus. I am trusty, I not for drinking. I thought you friend.

LUCIE   But I am your friend, Crebbs.

CREBBS   No. Is impossible to have meaningful relationship with vampire. You only after one thing.

LUCIE   No Crebbs, I want all of you, not just your blood.

She advances on him. He backs round the barrow.

LUCIE   I want your mind and your body too...

CREBBS   Nein...

LUCIE   Oh kiss me, Crebbs.

CREBBS   Nein…

LUCIE   The only thing that stands between us is… those things around your neck. Take them off, Crebbs.

CREBBS   Nein…

LUCIE   Come on, Crebbs…

CREBBS   Nein…

LUCIE   Get 'em off, Crebbs.

CREBBS   I do it! Ja.

He removes garlic and hurls it away.

LUCIE   (*Exhales.*)

CREBBS   You say kisses…

LUCIE   (*Exhales.*)

CREBBS   You say not just blood…

LUCIE   (*Exhales.*)

CREBBS   You say all of me…

LUCIE   (*Exhales. She is very close to him now.*)

CREBBS   …and you lie!

*As **Lucie** snarls and pulls back her head prior to fanging him, **Crebbs** whips a large crucifix from his back pocket and holds it up in front of her. Thunderclap. **Lucie** shrieks and turns a back somersault over a tomb. She cowers behind it.*

CREBBS   You think I born yesterday? You think I work for Dracula and not know what time day it is? I try be friends but you bite hand that feed you. You animal now. You dirt. You worse than lowest crawling thing now.

Lucie *bursts into tears.*

CREBBS   Is stop please. (*Offers her his hanky.*) You are taking please. (*Wiping nose.*) Stopping waterworks. I know is not your fault, you not help it. I sorry. You stop cry now. Hey, listen, maybe is not too late yet.

LUCIE What do you mean?

CREBBS You young, you strong, it take longer to work on you, this vampire thing. For me is different, I old, I tired, he bite, I finish, but for you, who knows? He drunken you how many time?

LUCIE Twice.

CREBBS Is two time is not so bad. Is important now, you drunken him yet?

LUCIE (*Appalled.*) No!

CREBBS Is good, is hope. After you drunken him is no hope. But now is maybe you get free of vampire thing if you good girl. Go much church.

Lucie shudders.

CREBBS Say much prayers.

Lucie shudders again.

CREBBS Come, we try. We are kneeling down together with crossifix.

Crebbs kneels beside tomb.

LUCIE I can't...

CREBBS You try please.

Lucie struggles to her knees beside him.

CREBBS Is good. Now we are putting hands together.

LUCIE No.

CREBBS Come, is not so hard. Is children do.

LUCIE It hurts... my hands.

CREBBS Come, try, come.

Lucie forces her hands together and locks her fingers.

CREBBS Is right! Is good! Is possible!

*Music. **Dracula** enters behind them and watches. They are unaware of his presence.*

Now we are praying please. Our Father…

LUCIE (*In pain.*) Ah… Ah…

CREBBS Which am in heaven…

LUCIE Art… Art…

CREBBS Try. Our father which am in heaven…

***Dracula** takes spade from wheelbarrow and creeps closer behind them.*

LUCIE No… No…

CREBBS Try… Try… Our Father which am in heaven…

LUCIE No! *Art* in heaven, it's our father which *art* in heaven!

CREBBS You say! You do! You be free!

***Dracula** snarls horribly as he raises spade. **Crebbs** turns but as he does so the hand holding the crucifix goes onto the tomb and **Dracula** brings the spade down and chops his hand off at the wrist. **Lucie** screams and runs to hide behind another tomb. Blood fountains out of **Crebbs'** wrist. **Dracula** grabs the stump and sucks on it as if it were an ice lolly, then transfers his fangs to **Crebbs'** neck and rips his throat out.*

***Lucie** tries to pick up the crucifix, which is still held by **Crebbs'** severed hand, but her hand shakes convulsively and can't touch it.*

***Dracula** watches her for a moment.*

DRACULA No, my dear, you may not. But do not be afraid. I have drunk deeply for you, now you shall be rewarded.

*He bares his wrist and bites it open. Black blood runs into his hand and drips off his fingers. He proffers his wrist to **Lucie**.*

DRACULA I give you life eternal in a sable stream and pleasure deep and dangerous. Do but drink.

LUCIE (*Gulps and swallows.*) No... please...

DRACULA What? Can you not scent it? See it, running in rivulets around my wrist? Come, drink.

LUCIE (*Pants but shakes her head.*)

DRACULA Warm to the touch but warmer yet to taste upon your lips. Drink!

LUCIE I... had rather... die.

DRACULA Ah! How wonderful it must be to be truly dead. That must be glorious, and yet men scrabble, weep and tear their fingers to the very bone to scrape a single day, a single hour beyond their time. If they but knew what you will shortly know... For you must be my sister and my bride, and if you will not drink from choice – yet you will drink!

He exhales loudly.

DRACULA Come!

***Lucie** is dragged towards him against her will.*

DRACULA Come!

***Lucie** keeps coming and falls to her knees in front of him. He moves his wrists close to her mouth.*

DRACULA Drink!

*Against her will, **Lucie's** top lip curls upwards and she begins to lower her mouth onto his wrist.*

VAN HELSING (*Off.*) This way!

DRACULA (*Snarls horribly.*)

Dracula gives *Lucie* a backhander that sends her flying. With the strength of twenty, *Dracula* rips the lid off the tomb, tosses *Crebbs'* body in and replaces lid. Turns towards *Lucie*, who staggers off. *Dracula* makes for the crucifix. It's heavy going for him and he snarls and hisses at it as he gets nearer. He manages to disengage it from *Crebbs'* hand which is left lying on the tomb.

VAN HELSING   (*Off, but nearer.*) Here, there are steps…

Dracula manages to pick the crucifix up.

DRACULA   It burns! It burns!

He holds it aloft as his hand bursts into flame, drops it and then plunges his hand into Crebbs' bucket of water, which immediately emits clouds of steam.

Van Helsing and *Seward* enter. *Van Helsing* carries a lantern and *Seward* a shotgun.

VAN HELSING   There!

Dracula looks up. *Seward* lets him have both barrels.

DRACULA   Fools!

Dracula raises his arms. There is a howling wind that blows all the lanterns out. Blackout.

SEWARD   Quick doctor.

Van Helsing relights lantern, and the enormous bat flies from where *Dracula* was standing, almost takes their heads off, and swoops over the audience and away.

VAN HELSING   Gone.

SEWARD   But I shot it.

VAN HELSING   Yes.

SEWARD   I couldn't have missed it that time, not if I'd tried.

VAN HELSING   No. It seems our bullets are useless against it.

SEWARD	Well, how do we kill it?
VAN HELSING	I don't know, Sir Robert. What is the time?
SEWARD	(*Checking watch.*) Two minutes past five.
VAN HELSING	So we have about half an hour to wait until dawn. The sun rose at 5.30am yesterday morning.
SEWARD	Let's hope we live to see it rise again.
VAN HELSING	Yes, for it may prove our greatest ally.
SEWARD	Eh?
VAN HELSING	The testament of Johannes Brucke, Sir Robert, 'It fear the goodly sun above all thing and only prey in hours of dark.'
SEWARD	Oh aye.
VAN HELSING	Where's Harker?
SEWARD	Harker? He was reet behind me. Harker! Where art th'lad?
HARKER	(*Off.*) I'm here.
VAN HELSING	It's all right, Mr Harker, it's gone.
HARKER	(*Off.*) Are you sure?
VAN HELSING	Yes. But there may be another entrance to this place. Be careful it doesn't get round behind you.
HARKER	(*Off.*) Agh! (*Rushes down steps.*) Oh my God, what are you trying to do to me woman? Why couldn't we stay up at the lodge? We could have locked the doors and kept it off somehow…
VAN HELSING	I did offer you the choice of staying in the lodge, Mr Harker.
HARKER	Yes. On my own. Ha! You'd like that wouldn't you? See Johnny nabbed by that… that thing. Oh yes, that's why you've dragged me up to this beastly castle, and now down into this… this…

VAN HELSING	We are here to look for your wife, Mr Harker.
HARKER	My wife? Ha! That's a laugh. I hardly know the stupid little dishrag, oh but I'm finding out aren't I, eh? Yes, this is loyalty for you, this is devotion, this is loving and honouring and obeying and with my body I thee worshipping isn't it? Ha!
SEWARD	What art th'talking about, Harker?
HARKER	Well she's run off hasn't she? She's left me, she's done a bunk. Oh my God, my God, what a mess. You two had better keep quiet about this, yes, you'd better keep your traps shut when we get out of here or... or else. My God, I'll be ruined if this ever gets out, I'll be a laughing stock, oh this'll go down a treat at the Club this will – 'Hullo Johnny old man, how's the missus? I hear she ran out on you on your honeymoon. With a bat.' Ha!
VAN HELSING	Mr Harker, I hardly think your wife's abduction can be described as 'running out on you'.
HARKER	That's right, stick together, oh you're all the same you blasted women. It's not fair. It's just not fair.

*He turns his back on them and sits on the tomb next to **Crebbs'** severed hand.*

SEWARD	Which way shall we go first?
VAN HELSING	No, Sir Robert, I rather think we must begin our search here.
SEWARD	Here? But Lucie's not here.
VAN HELSING	Let us hope not.

*She moves towards the tomb into which **Dracula** threw **Crebbs'** body.*

VAN HELSING	But there appears to have been some disturbance here recently.
SEWARD	You don't think...? Oh no...

*He moves to assist **Van Helsing**. They both push on the lid of the tomb, it moves slightly.*

SEWARD   Harker, give us a hand man.

HARKER   What?

SEWARD   Give us a hand.

HARKER   Oh. (*Notices **Crebbs'** hand beside him.*) Well, as it happens…

Holds it out to him. Realises what it is.

HARKER   Ahhhhhhhhhhhhhhhhhhhhh!

*Throws it up on the air. Catches it again by mistake. Juggles with it. Eventually he drops it, then hurls himself across the tomb that **Van Helsing** and **Seward** have half opened and dives inside it. Meanwhile **Seward** and **Van Helsing** rush to examine the hand.*

SEWARD   A hand!

VAN HELSING   But whose hand?

HARKER   (*Inside tomb.*) Ahhhhhhhhhhhhhhhhhhhh!

He emerges into view and crouches in the tomb, his hands covered in blood.

VAN HELSING   What is it Harker?

HARKER   Nanny?

SEWARD   Your hands man…

HARKER   Nanny? (*Rapidly.*) Once upon a time there were three bats and a girl called Lucie went to sleep and the Daddy bear said, 'Who's been sleeping in my bed', and the Nanny bear said, 'Who's been sleeping in my bed,' (*Rising falsetto.*) …and the little Johnny bear said, 'Who's been sleeping in my bed and she's still there!'

He has climbed out of the tomb and now bursts into

tears as he points into it. **Seward** *and* **Van Helsing** *rush across to heave the lid off completely.*

SEWARD   Crebbs.

VAN HELSING   Yes.

HARKER   Nanny?

SEWARD   His hand?

VAN HELSING   Yes.

HARKER   Johnny frightened.

SEWARD   I thought it were…

VAN HELSING   Yes.

HARKER   Johnny wants to come into your bed.

SEWARD   Look at his throat.

VAN HELSING   Yes.

HARKER   Johnny wet! (*He is.*)

VAN HELSING   (*Galvanising herself into action.*) Johnny mustn't worry, it doesn't matter. Now Johnny must try and be a good boy and go to sleep.

She leads him to another tomb and helps him onto it.

HARKER   Is this Johnny's bed?

VAN HELSING   Yes. (*Taking off her jacket.*) Now Nanny will tuck you in and come and see you in a few minutes. All right?

She tucks her jacket round him.

VAN HELSING   There. Now night-night.

HARKER   Sleep tight. (*Whimpers.*) Mind the bats don't bite.

VAN HELSING   No, no, night-night, sweet dreams.

HARKER   Treble times.

VAN HELSING   Treble times.

*As she moves away from him she sees the crucifix.
She picks it up.*

VAN HELSING 'A crucifix will hold it off and burn it while the hand be strong that holds it.'

SEWARD Poor Crebbs.

VAN HELSING Yes. What time is it now, Sir Robert?

SEWARD Ten past five.

VAN HELSING Another…

She hears a noise.

Who's there?

Seward *draws a pistol.*

SEWARD Come out. Is it…?

VAN HELSING We have the crucifix.

SEWARD Come out.

*Pause. Then **Mrs Crebbs** emerges from another burial chamber.*

MRS CREBBS I hear the shoutings. What you do here? Go quickly before…

SEWARD Mrs Crebbs, I…

VAN HELSING (*To **Seward**.*) Wait. (*To **Mrs Crebbs**.*) Before what, Mrs Crebbs? Before Count Dracula returns?

MRS CREBBS Is right.

VAN HELSING Because he… 'Because it will not eat nor drink of any natural food as common creature all will do, but ever seek its succour only in blood of human souls?' Because he is a vampire?

MRS CREBBS If you are knowing, why ask?

VAN HELSING Because I am curious to know why you should urge us to escape, when were we to do so we would undoubtedly try to ensure that you and your husband as well as the Count were dealt with by the relevant authorities.

MRS CREBBS I do not care anymore. I not want work for Dracula, but Jacov he say, 'Is work, we must do.' But I think he change now, we finish soon.

SEWARD Van Helsing, th'must tell her…

VAN HELSING Quiet.

HARKER Nanny?

VAN HELSING Quiet Johnny, I'm coming. Very well, Mrs Crebbs, should we ever get out of this place we will do all we can to mitigate your part in this… this hideous business. But tell us, where is Mrs Harker?

MRS CREBBS She not here?

VAN HELSING No.

MRS CREBBS Then she anywhere. Down here is tunnels, is miles tunnels. Is so big, I not know all. But Jacov know, maybe you ask Jacov.

VAN HELSING I wish we could, Mrs Crebbs.

Seward looks into tomb and shivers. Mrs Crebbs goes across to look. Music.

MRS CREBBS Oh Jacov, Jacov, I tell you, I say you, many time I say you. Why you no listen silly woman say we stop this work? Why? Why?

VAN HELSING Mrs Crebbs, your husband cannot hear you. He is dead.

MRS CREBBS (*Violently.*) What you know? You know all? You clever clever doctor you know life, all life, death, all death? You know nothing! Is life, yes? Is death, yes? Is all? No! Is ochsturn.

VAN HELSING Oh my God.

SEWARD What?

Van Helsing	Oh my God, undead.
Seward	What, you mean it's…
Van Helsing	Contagious. It means that he can transmit it to those he feeds upon, and that they in turn must be destroyed, or they too…
Mrs Crebbs	Ja. That is undead. You doctor, what is do. Speak. Tell.
Van Helsing	I don't know.
Mrs Crebbs	So what you know?
Van Helsing	Very little.
Mrs Crebbs	Nothing. You know nothing.
Van Helsing	Nothing.

Mrs Crebbs nods. She takes spade and rake from wheelbarrow, also a knife from her belt and proceeds to prise the handles from the tools and sharpen the ends of the handles.

Mrs Crebbs   Is undead. Is look like Jacov but is not. Is wake soon and be as him. As Dracula. Is need for destroy. These. (*The handles.*) Make sharp. Is one for Jacov, one for Dracula. (*To **Seward**.*) And is maybe one for your daughter. Is only way is nail down. Is need sharp wood, and is need hit. It need hit wood through body. Is either hit wood through heart or middle belly. Then is cannot rise again. Then is die. Is finish.

*She has sharpened the stakes to her satisfaction and hands them to **Van Helsing**.*

You hold please.

***Van Helsing** holds stake and **Mrs Crebbs** gets into tomb and guides it into position over where **Crebbs'** heart would be.*

Hold straight.

She strikes the top of the stake with the blade of the spade.

Hold straight! You doctor, you see much blood things, you hold straight.

*Mrs Crebbs strikes again. A groan from the tomb and smoke rises around **Mrs Crebbs** lit by a ghastly light from inside the tomb.*

VAN HELSING Stop! He's still alive!

MRS CREBBS Hold straight! Is not live! Is undead!

She strikes again and again and again, the clang of the spade interspersed with groans from the tomb. Then a scream, and silence as the light dies.

MRS CREBBS Is done. Is finish.

A pause.

SEWARD Mrs Crebbs, I don't know what to say but if there's owt you need, money or…

MRS CREBBS You not speak. I am knowing you. This your fault. You not come here Jacov is alive. Is you! Is you!

*Attacks him with her knife. They grapple. **Van Helsing** pulls **Mrs Crebbs** off. **Seward** levels pistol.*

VAN HELSING Don't shoot!

***Van Helsing** disarms **Mrs Crebbs**. **Seward** fires, **Mrs Crebbs** falls.*

VAN HELSING Why did you shoot?

SEWARD She had a knife, I thought… Is she…?

VAN HELSING Not yet, but she's dying.

She hears a noise.

Who's there?

***Lucie** enters.*

SEWARD Lucie! Thank God.

LUCIE   No, keep back. Keep away. I can't trust myself. Keep back. I came to warn you.

A heartbeat throbs.

He's coming.

VAN HELSING   Dracula?

LUCIE   Yes.

VAN HELSING   What time is it, Sir Robert?

SEWARD   Twenty-six minutes past five.

LUCIE   Help me, save me...

VAN HELSING   Quickly – outside. Harker, wake up!

*She wakes **Harker** who wails and clings to her. Music. Thunder.*

***Dracula** appears on the stairs, blocking their exit.*

DRACULA   Too late doctor. But I believe I have an appointment to view that brooch on your throat.

VAN HELSING   Keep off!

She raises crucifix in front of him. He snarls and hisses.

HARKER   No, Johnny want it, keep Johnny safe. Johnny have it!

*Grabs crucifix. He and **Van Helsing** struggle over it. It breaks in two pieces. **Dracula** laughs.*

You broke Johnny's crucifix...

DRACULA   Now, doctor...

VAN HELSING   The garlic, Sir Robert!

***Seward** pulls at **Mrs Crebbs'** necklace of garlic. She moans and holds onto it. The string breaks and it rolls all over the floor.*

SEWARD   It's brock! She's brock the bloody thing!

DRACULA   You see, doctor, it is useless. Come!

VAN HELSING   No...

DRACULA   Come!

VAN HELSING   No... please...

But she moves towards him against her will.

SEWARD   What art th'doing doctor?

DRACULA   Come!

VAN HELSING   I can't help it...

*She is close to **Dracula** now.*

DRACULA   Now doctor... (*Exhales.*) Your brooch...

***Van Helsing** takes choker off. **Dracula** caresses her neck. He howls like a wolf and is just about to sink his fangs into her when there is music, and a shaft of sunlight lights his face. He screams and leaps into the audience, snarling and fanging at them until he reaches the back row.*

The sun! the sun!

*Turns to see **Van Helsing** below him holding stake.*

You! You!

Spreads his arms, catches hold of a bar and abseils down over the audience's heads and impales himself on the stake through his stomach. The bloody end appears through his back. Still trying to fang her he pushes himself further and further onto the stake. Exhales and dies.

Silence.

LUCIE   He's gone. I felt him go, I felt his hold over me loosen and then lift. Daddy!

*Embraces **Seward**.*

VAN HELSING   Do you feel strong enough to walk, Mrs Harker?

LUCIE	Yes, I think so.
VAN HELSING	Then take your husband back to the lodge. There's no danger anymore. Keep him warm till I come.
SEWARD	Well, why don't we all go?
VAN HELSING	No, Sir Robert, we must attend to Mrs Crebbs.
SEWARD	Oh aye, you'll be all right, Lucie?
LUCIE	Yes. Come on, Johnny, come with me.
HARKER	Lucie?
LUCIE	Yes, come on, we'll go to bed now.
HARKER	Really? And will you read me a story?
LUCIE	But we're on our honeymoon, we can do more exciting things than that.
HARKER	What, you mean… you mean… we can have a pillow fight?
LUCIE	What?
HARKER	Oh come on, let's.

*They go. **Seward** stares down at **Dracula**.*

SEWARD	So. It's finished.
VAN HELSING	Not quite, Sir Robert. 'You not speak. I am knowing you. This your fault', Mrs Crebbs said. I wonder what she meant.
SEWARD	I have no idea. She was distracted, finding her husband like that… the shock.
VAN HELSING	Perhaps. But there are a number of aspects of this case that have puzzled me from the beginning. Transylvania seems an odd location to choose for a honeymoon – and you chose it, did you not, Sir Robert? Mr Harker, God help him, 'never liked the idea', he said so, and also said that after you received a letter from the Count, 'It had to be Transylballyvania didn't it?'

SEWARD   Well, I thought it'd be a change.

VAN HELSING   And is it not unusual for the bride's father to accompany her on the honeymoon?

SEWARD   Well, like I told Harker, I'm very fond of Lucie and...

VAN HELSING   Yes, all that might be quite plausible were it not for the sausage.

SEWARD   The sausage? What sausage?

VAN HELSING   The Seward and Browne's Original Recipe Smoked Sausage which the Count ate with such relish on our first meeting. For as I remember in the testament of Johannes Brucke there were clearly laid out a list of facts concerning the undead. And each and every one of those facts we have since proved to be true in every particular. With one curious exception. If my memory serves me correctly he wrote, 'It will not eat or drink of any natural food, as common creatures all will do, but ever seeks its succour only in blood of human souls'. And if you also remember I took the trouble to confirm that statement with Mrs Crebbs. Well, what are we to make of it? The Count certainly enjoyed and digested the sausage, so either poor Brucke and Mrs Crebbs were mistaken on this particular when they have been so manifestly correct on all other matters, or else the famous Seward and Browne Original Recipe Smoked Sausage is made of human blood.

SEWARD   Damn you, Van Helsing...!

VAN HELSING   Which would also account for the fact that according to Mr Harker, 'You spend half your life up to your armpits in offal because you won't let anyone know the secret of your precious recipe'. But somebody knew it, didn't they Sir Robert? Somebody guessed it simply by smelling one. And that somebody was Count Dracula. And he wrote you a letter telling you that in return for keeping your secret he wanted... What was it he wanted Sir Robert? It was your daughter wasn't it?

SEWARD No.

VAN HELSING And you brought her to him.

SEWARD No, I never dreamt he'd... I never knew what he was until... But whilst I were going up the castle with the sausages he must have flown straight down to the lodge and... and... but that doesn't matter any more. It's finished, Lucie's all right now. Thank you for saving my daughter, doctor, but now the time has come to pay your bill.

He raises pistol.

I'm sorry but you leave me no choice.

His finger tightens on the trigger, but before the gun goes off **Mrs Crebbs** *throws her knife at him. It embeds itself in* **Seward's** *chest. He falls.*

VAN HELSING *(To Mrs Crebbs.)* Thank you.

MRS CREBBS Is good.

She dies.

SEWARD Over here... Quickly, there's summat I must tell you.

VAN HELSING Lie still, Sir Robert, don't try to talk.

SEWARD No, I'm done for lass, but... the sausages...

VAN HELSING Lie still.

SEWARD No, I must tell you, when he wrote to me, Dracula, he said I must come and – I must bring him half a hundredweight of the sausages and I, God forgive me, I gave them to him. Some of them, enough, I couldn't carry them all but...

VAN HELSING	Well, now you have told me, lie still. Come, it's not important anymore if he had a store of your sausages.
SEWARD	No, you don't understand. He didn't want to eat them.

Music.

He wanted to contaminate them.

VAN HELSING	What?
SEWARD	I didn't understand at the time, because I didn't know then, what he was. He laughed at me and said, said they needed one more ingredient. And then he, he injected each sausage with a drop of his blood, and then, then he parcelled them up in three separate packages and made me seal and address them and then, and then he put them on the mail coach.
VAN HELSING	No! What were the addresses Sir Robert?
SEWARD	It's too late. They left last night…
VAN HELSING	The addresses, what were they?
SEWARD	Fortnum and Mason's, Harrods, and… Buckingham Palace.

Seward *dies.* **Van Helsing** *stands.*

VAN HELSING	What was it you said Sir Robert? 'They are eaten and enjoyed at every aristocratic dining table in England, including royalty'.

Music swells.

Poor England.

Blackout.

END OF ACT TWO

A C T I V I T I E S

Things to talk about

1 What was your first reaction when you read the title of this play? Talk about:

- what sort of things you expected of the play;

- whether the play turned out to be what you expected;

- what surprises you found in the way Chris Bond re-tells the famous story.

2 Re-read the first two pages of the play, up to the entrance of Crebbs. Jot down and talk about the different ways in which the playwright tells us:

- where the story is set;

- when it is set;

- to expect some horror and suspense;

- also to expect some humour;

- to realise straight away that Harker is not going to be the hero!

3 Brainstorm the titles of any horror films and stories you know.

- In pairs, try to put them into two lists:

  a) ones that rely on tension;
  b) ones that rely on special effects.

- What do you think makes a really good horror story?

- Which of these ingredients does this play have?

4 Read the first set of stage directions down to where Harker 'checks the doors and tentatively opens the trunk'.

- How easy is it for you to imagine what the room looks like from this description?
- What sort of atmosphere do you think Chris Bond is trying to generate for the audience with this opening?

Now look at the next stage direction in which Harker 'removes a string of sausages from the trunk with extreme distaste. A wolf howls sexily outside the French windows'.

- How do you suppose the audience will react when they see the string of sausages? Why?
- Why do you think the playwright has used the word 'sexily' to describe the wolf's howl?

5 Look carefully at the way Chris Bond has written the lines for Mr and Mrs Crebbs. Some would say that making fun of the way people talk is racist. What do you think?

Can you think of any other characters from, for example, television comedies which also use the way people speak to create comedy? Do you find these funny or offensive?

6 It would be hard to classify this play as a genuine 'horror' story, so how would you describe it?

Does this play remind you of any other plays or films you know? Talk about why you enjoyed them (or not).

7 **HARKER** *Why are you dressed up as a woman?*

VAN HELSING *Possibly because I am a woman.*

- In most accounts of the Dracula story Van Helsing is a man. Talk about what opportunities for comedy having Van Helsing as a woman presents.

Bram Stoker's novel *Dracula* is written as if it is Jonathan Harker's personal journal. His fiancée is called Mina, but she has a friend called Lucy who becomes one of Dracula's victims when he arrives in England. Harker helps put a stake through her heart before dashing off to Transylvania to rescue Mina.

- Do you think that it matters that these details have been changed?

- Do you know of any other plays or films that are quite different from the original novels?

- Talk about what reasons playwrights might have for altering the original stories.

THINGS TO WRITE ABOUT

8 *The lodge has recently been converted into a bijou holiday dwelling.*

Take a look at some examples of travel brochures and study the kind of language they use to describe villas.

Write a description of this one. You will need to try and make the place sound very attractive, but how will you deal with the local wildlife and strange neighbours?

9 On pages 27–28, Van Helsing reads aloud the letter by Johannus Brucke.

- Imagine that another similar letter is found elsewhere in the lodge. Write your own message on it.

- Present your work so that it could be used as a *prop* in a stage production.

10 During the play we discover that Seward and Browne's Original Recipe Smoked Sausage is 'eaten and enjoyed at every aristocratic dining table in England, including royalty'.

- Design an advertisement for these sausages which might appear in a high class glossy magazine.

- Now you know what the 'secret ingredient' of the sausages is, what do you suppose Chris Bond is suggesting about aristocrats?

- Write the headline and opening paragraph of a newspaper report which reveals the truth about both the sausages and the people that eat them!

11 Imagine that Dr Tanya Van Helsing applies for a post at another university. How might she use this experience in her application letter?

12 Read the scene on pages 18–19 in which Van Helsing sets up a blood transfusion. Chris Bond develops a *running joke* here by having a wolf howl every time the word 'blood' is mentioned. He gets an extra laugh by having the actors *double take* at the end of the sequence: ('They all turn to listen. Silence.') Another example of a running joke is when Harker doesn't understand what Crebbs means by 'mein Herr' on pages 11–12.

- In groups, read through one of these scenes again. Talk about how it works. Try the scene out for yourselves, concentrating on getting the timing of the lines and movements right.

- Devise a short scene of your own in which a running joke is set up so that the audience thinks it knows what will happen next but, in fact, it doesn't.

13 Jot down at least four lines which show the different sides of Harker's character. Do the same for Lucie. Practise saying them aloud and put a good clear action with each one. Think about exactly what you are trying to tell an audience by delivering the lines in this way.

14 Set out a performance space in the classroom or studio. Choose any character from the play and take it in turns to step into the performance space and say, in a 'style that's big and bold', who you are. The aim of the exercise is to make it immediately clear to an audience what sort of person you are playing, so, think about:

- how you walk on;

- how you will sit or stand when you arrive;

- how you look at the audience;

- the tone, volume and pace of your voice, and perhaps also your accent.

Having introduced yourself in character in this way, devise a short monologue that would tell an audience a bit more. Chris Bond's advice is to 'look for the obsession', so Seward's talk might start with something like this:

Seward's the name and sausages is me game. I love 'em. There's nowt like the feel of offal slipping between yer fingers...

15 In pairs or small groups, choose a short section of the play (just twelve lines or so) and rehearse them trying to capture the 'big, bold style'. This doesn't simply mean over-acting them, but rather making it absolutely obvious what the character is like, and showing clearly what they are feeling.

STAGING THE PLAY

16 In the original production of *The Blood of Dracula*, Mr and Mrs Crebbs were played by the same actor. What would be the advantages and disadvantages of casting the play like this?

17 When does an audience's experience of theatre actually start? When the lights go down in the auditorium, or before that? It might start from the moment you see a poster advertising the play. It can be developed when you buy your ticket, and the programme might also add to the fun and atmosphere. In the original production the programme notes were printed on a large sheet of paper which included instructions on how to fold it into a crucifix. The audience were advised to do this just in case Dracula came rampaging amongst them!

Design either a programme or poster (maybe even

a ticket) that would suit this play and add to the fun of it. You will obviously need to think about the style of the play, but consider also what essential information you need to give and what additional information might be interesting and useful.

18 Jot down some ideas for other things that would make going to watch this play more fun. For example:

- how might you decorate the entrance foyer?

- what music could you use to *underscore* different parts of the play?

- how might the ushers and usherettes be costumed and how might they treat the audience?

- what special food and drink could you have in the interval?

19 The play certainly presents a few technical problems. Chris Bond describes how a 'low tech' solution to some of these might be found:

All the sound effects and music etc. can be made live on stage by the performers. One way of doing this is to have additional members of the cast dressed as 'gargoyles'. They could be cloaked and hideously masked and flank the massive fireplace in the lodge. These performers could then make the basic noises of the show and move the bats around the stage on the end of thin rods. This would work particularly well if the bats were painted in special paint which picked up ultra-violet light: during the bat scenes, the main lights would be taken down and U.V.s put on so the audience would only see the bats and not the performers moving them.

The large bat could be pulled along a nylon wire stretched between the window and the fireplace. Its movement along the wire would cause it to bounce, giving the impression that its wings were flapping. Its appearance from the chimney can be disguised by puffing an amount of Fullers earth through the opening from backstage (don't use real soot – it would be impossible to clean up!) The art is to create so much movement and confusion that the audience will not see how the trick is played.

In Act Two, the gargoyles could become effigies on the tombs, statues, or indeed gargoyles!

What other technical problems would you see in staging this play? Describe how you might tackle one of them.

THE VAMPIRE BUSINESS

The legend of the vampire goes back further than anyone can really say. Virtually every country has some sort of story about such creatures. They are said to exist in the forests of Mexico, while in Indian, Greek and Roman mythology you can find tales of men who ravish young women and feed off their blood.

Some people have gone quite mad with the idea of vampires. A group of soldiers were sent to one town in the Balkans to investigate reports of vampirism, and later signed statements describing how they had found corpses, apparently full of fresh blood, dug from their graves and staked through the heart.

Many versions of the story (including Bram Stoker's novel) are really quite sexy. Some psychologists have tried to explain the stories by saying that people fear sex in the same way as they fear death. Put sex and death together and you have two powerful ingredients for a thriller.

The story we know as *Dracula* can be traced quite accurately:

1456 Vlad Tepes, known as Vlad the Impaler, acquired a fearsome reputation by dealing with his enemies by impaling them, then eating his dinner while he watched them die. His father was known as Vlad Dracul (Vlad the Devil). At one time he owned Bran Castle, which has since become the model for the dark and forbidding fortress we associate with Dracula.

1560 Countess Elizabeth Bathory was born. You may not have heard of her, but her exploits added quite a bit to later stories of vampires. She was responsible for the torture and murder of up to 600 young women. She bathed in their blood, believing it would keep her young-looking. Eventually she was bricked up in her own castle. Being a member of the aristocracy it wasn't thought proper to execute her.

1816 Lord Byron met fellow poet Percy Shelley and his new wife Mary. During a pretty wild gathering at an Italian villa, Mary created the story of *Frankenstein*, and Byron is said to have made up a story called *The Vampyre*, which was later written up and published by...

1819 ...his companion John Polidori. In this story the vampire is a charming and seductive aristocrat called Lord Ruthwen. The description of him makes him very similar to Lord Byron (who also had a hungry interest in young women).

1820 J.R. Planche, a leading writer of Victorian melodramas, adapts a French play called *Le*

Vampire. Planche wanted to set his play in Romania, but the theatre that took it on had lots of Scottish costumes in store at the time, so they set it there!

1847 An adaptation of the story was serialised in popular weekly installments. It was called *Varney the Vampire* and ran to over 800 pages.

1897 Bram Stoker publishes *Dracula*. Stoker worked in the theatre and probably knew Planche's play.

20 Read this scene from the melodrama by J.R. Planche. The play starts in a cave in Scotland where Lady Margaret has fallen asleep on a tomb after becoming lost. The tomb belongs to a vampire called Lord Ruthven. Unless he can 'marry' a virgin before the moon sets on the following night his reign of terror will end. This how the play ends:

RUTHVEN (*Furiously.*) Margaret, we are waited for.

RONALD Barbarian! I forbid the ceremony. You have no right over her – I am her father.

LADY M. You are – you are my loving, tender father: – I will not wed against his will.

RUTHVEN I'll hear no more! – she is my bride betrothed: this mad-man would deprive me of her.

RONALD (*Loud thunder: Another gust of wind blows open the casement.*) See! See! the moon already rests upon the wave! – One moment! – but one moment!...

RUTHVEN Nay, then thus I seal my lips, and sieze my bride.

Ruthven draws his poignard: rushes on Ronald – Robert throws himself between Ruthven and Ronald, and wrenches the dagger from his grasp.

LADY M. Hold! hold! – I am thine; the moon has set.

RUTHVEN And I am lost!

A terrific peal of thunder is heard; Unda and Ariel appear; a thunderbolt strikes Ruthven to the ground, who immediately vanishes. General picture.

THE CURTAIN FALLS

- How does the style and language of this play contrast with Chris Bond's version?

- *The Vampire* was a great success when it was first staged, but how do you think modern day audiences would react to it? Can you explain your answer?

The first film version of the story was made in Germany in 1922 by the great director F. W. Murnau. It was called *Nosferatu,*and although the names of the characters and places were changed it was so similar to Bram Stoker's novel that his widow was able to sue the film-makers for breach of copyright. The makers of the 1930 version starring Bela Lugosi didn't make the same mistake. The image we still tend to have of Dracula as clean shaven and having staring eyes and slicked-back hair comes from that film, but compare that with Bram Stoker's description:

His face was strong – a very strong – acquiline, with a high bridge of a thin nose and peculiarly arched nostril; with lofty domed forehead, and hair growing scantily round the temples, but profusely elsewhere. His eyebrows were massive, almost meeting over the nose, and with bushy hair that seemed to curl in its own profusion. The mouth, so far as I could see under the heavy moustache, was fixed and rather cruel looking, with peculiarly sharp white teeth; these protruded over the lips whose remarkable ruddiness showed astonishing vitality in a man of his years. For the rest, his ears were pale and at the tops extremely pointed; the chin was broad and strong, and the cheeks firm though thin.

21 Look at these titles from other Dracula films. (They are all genuine!)

Dracula's Daughter; Brides of Dracula; Son of Dracula; Dracula – Prince of Darkness; Dracula has Risen From the Grave; Taste the Blood of Dracula; The Satanic Rites of Dracula; Countess Dracula; Dracula AD 1972; Blacula.

- Read the *blurb* on the back cover of this book. talk about the purpose of this sort of writing and how it works.

- Make up blurbs for two of the films listed above.

22 Brainstorm as many other depictions of Dracula as you can. His images has been used as the basis for cartoon characters and many adverts for everyday products.

- Why do you think the character has become so popular both as a figure of horror and of fun?

- The Romanian tourist board are trying to 'clean up' the legend of Vlad Tepes. If you lived in that area of Romania would you want them to?

23 Look back to the first few pages of Act Two (pages 36–37) in which Crebbs is explaining to Lucy how to become a good vampire. Imagine that there is such a thing as a school for vampires.

- Work on your own to devise a monologue for a teacher in such a school. What would they say to their new class?

- Work in groups to improvise a scene between some students at the school who are struggling with a particular homework that they have been set.

24 Presumably, after eating a few Seward and Browne sausages which have been contaminated by Dracula, people would start craving for more human blood.

- Improvise a scene which shows someone, or some people, beginning to thirst for blood but not understanding what is happening to them.

- Work through the scene again but this time try to capture a sense of horror as people realise that something awful is happening to them but they can't do anything about it.

25 According to various superstitions your chance of becoming a vampire increase if:

you commit suicide

were born on Christmas Day

eat the meat of a sheep killed by a wolf

your mother was watched by a vampire

a cat steps on your coffin

you happen to be the seventh son of a seventh son.

Vampires apparently meet once a year on St Andrew's Eve (November 29th).

- In groups, improvise the meeting. You might start your social chit-chat by explaining to each other how you came to be one of the undead!

- What sort of things might be on the agenda for such a meeting? The poor reputation of vampires? The woeful lack of virgins in some areas? What sort of proposals and resolutions would you make?

Of course, vampires can be dealt with. If you have one in your area you could try:

- placing grains of incense in his coffin – it won't destroy him but apparently he'll nibble on this when he wakes up, which will delay him leaving the dungeon;

- stuffing garlic in his mouth (not very popular with anyone really);

- burying him face downwards (which may cause a problem in Australia eventually);

- frighten him away with a large black dog with an extra pair of eyes painted on top of its head (don't ask me why – it's just a legend!).

If you only suspect that there is a vampire around you are advised to find a young girl and have her ride a horse over all the local graves. If the horse refuses to step over one you'll know that's where the vampire is.

26 Imagine that a modern day local council is worried that they might have a vampire in the area. They call in an expert who is full of those kinds of ideas.

Write a short script of their meeting. Use the list below, and your knowledge of the characters in Chris Bond's play, as a guide for your own characters. Give them names that you think say something about them.

Chairman of the Council: a blunt, down-to-earth, sceptical businessman.

The expert: calm, educated, scientific – but always prepared to realise that even scientists don't know all the answers to mysterious things.

The local policeman: out of his depth. Happier using teddy bears to demonstrate playground safety to 5-year-olds than dealing with gory murders.

The tea lady or caretaker: seems to have a particular interest in recent events. Blessed with old wisdom and strange personal habits!